Love...

Life's Illusive

Zenith

By Dudley (CHRIS) Christian

A

Pause For Poetry ©

Publication

Acknowledgement:

With all my heart, I dedicate this book to my wife, Grace Ursula born: May 16 1941, married: Sept 18 1967, died: May 23 1997 (cancer).

Also, to my children Noel Alston, Dudley Ziegfried, and Leilani Teresa, whose presence and diligence in their own lives and acknowledgements gave me the strength and reason to continue through the hardest struggles of my life... Thank you

Special thanks to my current wife, Marilyn Christian for compiling, organizing and finalizing the books of my collections. Her photographing and editing skills were vital to all of my works.

ISBN: 978-0-9877501-2-9

First Edition February 2012
Revised Edition June 2017

Cover Photograph: Beach at Tulum, Mexico © Marilyn Christian

An Opening Word by the Author...

Many people often ask:

"How do you write and do you have to often rewrite your material?"

I have long summed up my answer to the above with the following:

"A Word, the written word, small purveyor of a thought, so like a thought, once thought, cannot be recalled, so too, a word once writ, should need NOT be re-written, for with such licence, we would but change ... the very substance of the thought."

... DNC © 1970

Dudley (Chris) Christian founded and hosted the first and only "PAUSE FOR POETRY" show dedicated solely to the introduction of new and unknown poets and their works. This TV series ran from 1974 to 1985.

Table of Contents

Dear Reader:

...This book is a compilation of Life, Love, Past and Present expressions of many of the times which I lived thru and learned from. It is an attempt to catalogue many of what may have been my mistakes or just my regrets.

...To say THANK YOU to those who helped me walk those roads and collect those threads of Life and Love, to those who walked out of my life on seeing their hoped-for conclusions lost, or their plans for a future dashed, as I walked alone and went on my path. Let me illuminate or clarify where I was sent on my solitary journey of self-discovery...

...In these verses, I revisit places and countries, I see again past lives I was so much a part of and which, in some ways, I wish I could have remained in. In this walk thru my life, you will find me often times reminiscing and trying to recapture the Good times and knowing that I shall NEVER be able to relive those times.

I can only repeat... Thank You...

...So come along to take a look at the shadow of death as it approached me, but was rejected, when " 'Twas Midnight on a Moonlit Eve" (page 48) and realize that " 'Tis those who are of Death Afraid" (page 56) concludes my awakening...

I Close My Eyes

I close my eyes...

And I design...

Deep within the reaches

Of my mind...

A Spread of leaves...

On a bed of clay...

With a head of moss...

For you on to lay...

So near besides me in unison

As the twittering birds fly overhead

The shy deer pauses us by

As it stops to feed

Content they and we

One with Nature

As the whisper of the winds

Caressingly passes overhead

Songs soft to you of devotion

Cast out for thine ears alone...

Then Sun It Set Into the West

Then Sun it set into the West

Another day it beckoned rest

While yet my Heaven it endured

Your fragrance lingered near

Natural perfume of your hair

Which flows upon my shoulder

Where for nights rest

You lay your head

Then morning's light brought life

Such as I had of but dreamed

For vision mine of memory

'Twas real with You beside me

Fulfilled I felt like unbeknown

Before had been I in life

So all was right...

And bright...

And Happiness itself

It blossomed forth for me

For me who had on life glanced

With but dark dismal despair

A smile from deep deep within

From deep within the heart of mine

Burst forth to outwards openness

To spread to linger and to play

In warmth upon the lips

That you had kissed...

So tenderly with Love...

Elaine Elaine

Endless eternity is too short

Life's length is not long enough

After all time -- yet there remains

Immortal Indestructible feelings

Newborn Neverending deep feelings

Encompassing Embraceable -- You.

18 June 1980

I Walked By...

I walked by...

You turned and you brushed me

For the shortest of moments in time

Your body my body contacted

And the fleeting moment 'twas mine

Your aura surrounding projected

Merged with mine in perfect accord

Your fragrance and presence fulfilling

Each dream man didst ever afford

So -- I reached out...

Like wisp of the wind in the air

For to hold to that moment together

Alas moving swift -- you weren't there

Visions appear in the eyes view

Dreams haunt the sleeping at times

Yet 'twas a short wakeful moment

When you appeared to be mine

And -- I'll be waiting

'Til your commitments are through

'Til your fans and your attractions

No longer are calling to you

'Til the last dawning of sunlight

'Til the last star fall and die

'Til for but a short moment remembered

You'll come once again passing by.

Your Youthful Eyes Met Mine

Your youthful eyes met mine

I froze...

My years of Emptiness

Flashed by...

My life renewed

It blossomed hope...

And Cynical I

In Love

Believed again

Hi Hiker -- Come Rest Awhile and Rap

Hi Hiker -- come rest awhile and rap

Let me your hidden self in enter

Nay, not alone... For I too myself shall share

Why should our lives so different

Cause us to gaze each other on

As beings each from other worlds

When but Humans simple all are we

There now a smile, a friendly word

And we can chat away our Fears

Across the abyss of unfamiliarity

Until there naught remains

'Tween us except our friendliness

Trust, Honesty and a genuine warmth

A warmth that grows in hearts

In lone and lonely hearts

Which wonder on in quest of life

In quest of what could one day be

Or yet mayhap of what has been

And fast the miles roll on and on

As alas you turn to me and smile

Reaching for a scrap of crumpled paper

You write your name and number

Then passing it towards me ever shyly

You wink as you prepare to leave

And wish that we a moment more could spend

O'er a cold Coke inside the near McDonald's

Then you are gone Hitchhiker gone and I

Alone, alone again am I in solitude

So driving 'round four blocks I then return

To sit alone and sip from McDonald's flavours

When suddenly you light besides me

And You Smile...

And fill my day and life with joy

at your presence...

Memories Are Roads We've Traveled

Memories are roads we've traveled

Scenes we stopped to gaze upon...

Hillsides which in their deep splendour

Held long our longing there to part belong

Memories are eagles high in flight

High, higher than the tallest spire of trees

Free, floating lone and majestic in beauty

Now here then like a flash forever gone

Memories are mountain streams we watched

As we above them stood in awesome wonder

Looking down to their minuscule sizes

As we agreed to higher yet some peak attain

And great the quest we set upon it seems

As unfamiliar woods and grounds we cover

Memories are slippery mossy rocks and trees

Now barren and dry by the prolonged sunshine

Of a bounteous and seemingly never-ending summer

A summer which has brought us first together

Memories are bees which buzzed our feet

And stayed to savour all the snacks we shared

As we prepared to wander into the unknown

Two seeming strangers we in search each other of

Memories are yellow, green and red and gold

The leaves upon the ground where rested you

While in the trees above the unseen chirping

Of a bird is heard and rustle of the wings

As grouse and pheasant take to flight

And we in silence of each other's hearts

We so quiet remain that the shy deer

It pauses unbeseen by us to eat in leisure

Then moves on at peace with us and nature

Unafraid these creatures of the humans wild

They gaze upon we two as we make memories

Memories to call upon in times of total loneliness

To reach out for fulfillment of in joy

Until we as one united in loves garden

Like Eve and Adam alone we with nature

Unashamed and uncaring of the world

Of All its taboos and its useless rules

Which hide from us the truth of love and joy

Which keep from us the serenity of peace

Which shackles us with its age-old morality

That would but keep us miserable and alone

And let us live our empty drab and oh...

So well cut lives...

As our ancestors did...

And as their peers or ours...

They who would have us live...

To be but cogs in the wheel of life

And be no more than they have been...

And even that alas sans memories

Sans sweet memories of love...

<u>To Every Part There Is a Player</u>

To every part there is a player

To every heart there is a lover

To every life there is a reason

To every cause there is a price

Let then this player play his part

Let then this heart be thy lover

Let then my life see you as a reason

Let then the price of your cause

Be my love

A Year Has Come Again and Gone

A year has come again and gone

The Seasons all have passed

Until the warmth of Summer 'n' Spring

Has shared with us their last

Birds like flowers drifted

In beauty 'neath our skies

Then slowly disappeared from view

To bid their fond goodbyes

Yet lingering deep within our hearts

We keep there fond memories

Of what has been, of those we met

As this year we've walked life's street

It's this alone that us sustains

As older e'er we grow

The beauty of the times gone on

Warmth of friends we've come to know

So friend, tho short our rendezvous

Full filled, as we wished, it's been

With joys such as we chose to share

Be it shared with women or with men

Then let our past year be recalled

With all its frolic and its fun

And may the days and months ahead

Be but each a brand new one

May all we've hoped but did not find

In the future full prove true

But above it all may we e'er recall

Friendship shared between we two...

Canada -- truly a land

of beautiful flowers and beautiful women

-- Alas --

Un sans fragrancé et un sans chaudement

I Wish Not to Possess Thee

I wish not to possess thee

Just as man might wish a woman to possess

To have and hold closely

For thy body alone

But rather I would but put thee to sleep

Beneath the glow of the summer's moon

Caressed by the murmuring waves

Beating upon some quiet secluded seashore

And hold you nestled naked in my arms

Your pillow for the night my inner shoulder

Your blanket for warmth my body

Your nightdress naught

But the sweet fragrance of yourself

Then awaken could I at morning's light

As golden sunbeams filter thru your hair

And watch would I a new day dawning

When in your mirror-like eyes I gaze

A lasting vision therein to soft behold

A recall of the night we'd known

A picture clear of the very soul you own

Which with me for a space in time you shared

You made my life of emptiness complete

This then an enchanted evening was

Which blossomed from a budding flower

A flower which first thine eyes in I beheld

While unto thee I said sincerely

I wish not to possess thee

Just as man might wish a woman to possess

To have and hold closely

For thy body alone

But rather I would but put thee to sleep

Beneath the glow of the summer's moon

Two Lonely Strangers On the Street

Two lonely strangers on the street

Perchance one time did meet

And grew acquainted they 'fore long

As evening passed and night on drew

Yet on and on their friendship grew

Contented unaware of time long gone

When darkness fell upon the land

Night's passage start to take command

Together they agreed the time to spend

Then they in unplanned rendezvous

Sought shelter in the night for two

A perfect way a perfect day to end

They talked and frolicking did play

They laughed and joked the hours away

There in each other's arms nestled warm

In unison as one they moved

Secure for now that they were loved

And ne'er would the other to bring harm

So beautifully the night passed by

To awaken refreshed at mornings light

While near outside the happy songbirds sang

All echoes clear of what had been

Renewed their feelings warm again

And the sounds of love once more together rang

Sunlight... a new day filtered in

To caress and shine upon them dim

Locked in the eyes each other of as they lay

Two people now who owned the world

No more just lonely boy and girl

No more the strangers they of yesterday

But life is crude and life is cruel

Yet seems we must play by its rules

They too alas fate'd planned to steer apart

Would what had been gone on and on

Or be forgot when one was gone

To remain but treasured memories of the heart

Two lonely strangers they had been

Who came together, parting friends

Each out life's destiny to pursue

Deep feelings hid within each now stirred

Confusion rampant in him in her

Uncertainty of what now they'd do

'Twas life and fate and destiny

Combined to change their Itinerary

Combined to offer each a different life

Can they now return to what has been

Will he forget her or she forget him

Or meet again to brave life's bitter strife

Look back, look back in love and joy

Forget a moment which did annoy

And weigh instead the happiness full shared

Your thoughts alone of what has been

Can retain the beauty we have seen

For those hours -- short -- ours -- because we cared

They're gone, you're gone, and I remain

Your form and fragrance e'er lingering

In dreams, you too will one day see

We all are strangers at the start

But age old friends deep in the heart

Unable we to change loves destiny

So it's your choice which must be made

To look back with joy or back ashamed

At being full the angel life did you plan

The greatest gift that two can share

In contented bliss it's rich and rare

And this was ours as woman and as man

Two lonely strangers on the street

Perchance by destiny did meet

And life that had passed us by...

It called us in...

With Lithe a Body As Man Did E'er Behold

With lithe a body as man did e'er behold

And like a trembling captive bird

You came to me in body -- mind -- and soul

The beating fast of thy heart I heard

While warm and near to me safe you nestled.

Feather-like soft and warm as down

Your fingers did my face caress

Your arms did my body full surround

While breath-like felt I did

Your lips against mine press

The unison of two made complete.

This was the cloud thru which we flew

This was the heaven which I entered in

This was the moment which we shared

This our first embrace -- our love's beginning

This our elusive quest which was o'er

This our ultimate triumph o'er loneliness' power

And we became as one -- and we were glad.

Then light of dawning took the aura away

We once again realities must face

Tho once again they body warm did lay

Pressed close to mine in perfected space

There where it seemed 'twas meant to be

Like unfeathered struggling bird in safety nest

Which fell to Earth from safety's highest tree

Which fell yet stayed content -- tho in unsure fear

Afraid to full accept the safe new love offered here

And waited 'til but feathers you had grown

Skyward and away flew back you to your own...

Tiny Teardrops from the Angels

Tiny teardrops from the angels
Fall upon the winters ground
Cold and wet yet sweet and softly
They seem to grace the world around.

Why are you crying in the Heavens
What causes pray brings you dismay
Who has hurt or you offended
Oh Angels why cry you today.

The Sun is shining 'mongst the grey clouds
Tho half its warmth Winter recalls
Still just for you tulips are blooming
Robins sing your praise in song.

Lovers hold hands walking slowly
Looking aback to yesternight
When together they kissed softly
'Neath clear blue sky's starlight

Now then why is it you're crying
Why doth thy soft teardrops fall
Surely one heart like mine new broken
Could not upset you so at all

Oh Angel soft of heart for lovers
Your tears may yet my love recall
Once she's seen your tiny teardrops
Which for love you free let fall.

Your heart's of gold and ever open
Your arms must hold the Universe
For mortal man cannot imagine
What pain would cause your tear's outburst.

Then cry Angel of the morning
Your sweet tears will fill my life
To renew love I felt was fleeting
And make again it all seem right.

Teardrops fall from Heavens Angels
Soft as rain on Winter's ground
But these which fall are for the growing
Of love and life for lovers all.

Tiny teardrops from the angels
Fall upon the Winter's ground
Cold and wet yet sweet and softly
They grow the seeds that love casts 'round.

7/3/81

Is This Not Then the Ultimate

Is this not then the ultimate

To laugh at life and years

To feel alive within the arms

Which dries away the tears

Which draws us to each other

Consoling our deep fears

For such was mine a moment

A short shared space of time

Now really alone and empty

You've left these arms of mine

Is this not then the ultimate

The beauty of two to see

So deep in love each other with

That naught else matters we

Save being with and being one

To silent rush to bare oneself

While watching them bare too

To reach out then each other for

To share content together

Love's sweet rendezvous.

Once a Man With a Wife of 18 Years

Once a man with a wife of 18 years

Met a girl with an age of 18 years

And he felt for the first time in 18 years

That his life was again like at 18 years

So he came up and said to the 18 year

That his heart burst with love for 18 years

Now it flowed free when near to her 18 years

And he'd leave now his wife of 18 years

So he courted in words sweet the 18 year

Lavished on her gifts fine for an 18 year

Tried to please each whim of this 18 year

Hoping she'd be mature for her 18 years

But then said unto him this 18 year

I'm afraid if you leave wife of 18 years

That we too would not last for 18 years

For you're alas e'en now twice my 18 years

By the time that I've reached twice 18 years

You'd be then three times my 18 years

And I'm not sure if after those 18 years

You'll still see me as you do at 18 years

Then the man with the wife of 18 years

Brokenheartedly said goodbye to miss 18 year

Thought of life he had wasted for 18 years

Said goodbye too to wife his of 18 years

Not too long met another of 18 years

Who told not to him she was 18 years

But they courted and laughed like two 18 years

Cared she not he was older by 18 years

'Fore the year passed he married the 18 year

Then he found that she really was 18 years

But matured she indeed was for 18 years

More a woman than his wife past of 18 years

Soon a child was borned by the 18 year

And a family fast grew they for 18 years

'Til she'd doubled in years full her 18 years

Still they loved like when she was an 18 year

One day met they a woman twice 18 years

All alone said she'd been now for 18 years

Spoke to the man who had loved her at 18 years

When she'd thought him too old for her 18 years

Now she wished she could call back 18 years

For she knew now time is short for an 18 year

And it would matter not he was twice her 18 years

If she could only be loved like at 18 years

Then they told her they'd been married for 18 years

And recalled he how he loved her at 18 years

When she said he was too old for her 18 years

Tho he then was but twice times her 18 years

But now he'd loved this other for full 18 years

Who like she had been then just an 18 year

'Cept she was matured for her 18 years

Became a wife, woman, mother o'er the 18 years

And deep inside had grown his love for the 18 years

For his wife here now besides him for 18 years

And he'd ne'er leave his true love of 18 years

Tho they both live to ten times the 18 years

Hard the lesson that was taught the first 18 year

She who thought age mattered most back at 18 years

Threw away love of one twice her 18 years

Lived alone and unloved now for 18 years

When if only she had thought back 18 years

He offered her love true when she was but 18 years

The Lion Roams His Kingdom Wide

The Lion roams his kingdom wide

In search of prey his mate has been

To seek out hunt down and destroy

Is to her but life's sweet game

Her master roars and listens she

To this her king of all the land

Now but a playful furry cat

Snuggles safe besides her man

Then he's away and she must rule

Put up a front as being strong

Protective now unto her death

Unafraid to ever challenge wrong

Yet deep within she too fear feels

When she finds herself alone

A Thought... A Wish...

An I remember You...

Today and ALL year through...

Orin MacLaughlin Goodbye

'Orin Mac' Goodbye

Goodbye from we who knew you

You lived as so many want to

Full, free and hard and fast

Until life could not keep pace

Until help was sought to stay you

Until Death before you stood

And there it placed an empty void

For you to walk or fall deep into

For such was your life

For such was your life

Your way of living fully

Each day, each thing, each thought

You didn't die oh Orin Mac

You, nay, not as they wouldst have us think

You did not die, for it wasn't you

You ran too hard and fast in life

To simply sit and let it run out on you

Nay you could not then have died

But rather you the void of death

Would enter into ever willingly

And mayhap therein you again

Run on as even in life you did

Until you had yourself -- burnt out

Burnt out

Burnt to a different seeming state

Wherefrom we mere mortals cannot move

Wherefrom your voice we hear not

Yet we who knew you Orin Mac

We know that tho you're gone

You did not die

You did not die as mortal man

You did not sit and let life flee

For in you burned too hot the energy

The energy to be and move and love

And this is life is it not

So though mayhap you did burn out

'Twas but within the grasp of mortal thought

'Twas but thine own doing

And surely not the cold and clammy

The slow and waiting hands of death

That brought thee down

We know

We all who knew you Orin Mac

We say goodbye for you are gone

But choice of time we know was thine

You left us as you choose

So Goodbye Orin Mac

Goodbye from we who knew you

We know we'll meet again

For our paths you guided in the past

And mayhap in the future you

You have but gone to them prepare

A Toast to You and Yours Today

A toast to you and yours today

May health and happiness go your way

May you endure the test of time

And all you seek may you soon find

May skies be blue to bless your life

May you know not want know not strife

And as with these you are blessed

May you share the wealth with all the rest

A helping hand to one who's down

Thoughtful words and beaming smile

Laughter in amongst the tears

Warmth and hope thruout the years

For few are blessed as you may be

And fewer yet know serenity

For forgetful they when at their best

Shared not their wealth with all the rest.

'Tis Simple What I Do

'Tis simple what I do

To promote poetic art

I strive to find the hidden

Talents lurking in the dark

I light the lonely corners

Where a wealth of words lie hid

From closet to cookie jar

Try I to open every lid

Still to me 'tis quite simple

And my contributions small

Yet at my paying labours

It's not seen as such at all

For to them my contributions

And weekly appearances all say

Here's one who lends a hand

To help others on their way

And fine by them I'm treated

No matter who they are

For small tho be my functions

To their eyes I am a star

Smile, Smile Oh Lips

Smile, smile oh lips

While deep inside my heart it cries

Smile oh lips

Your movements keep my eyes dry

Smile oh lips

Show not the world inside me

Smile oh lips smile

Smile that my loneliness no one shall see

Speak, speak oh lips

In frolic words and phrases cast

Speak oh lips

As slowly hours alone I pass

Speak oh lips

Confess not truths you know

Speak oh lips speak

But break not confidence you hold

Reach out, reach out arms

Grasp -- reach -- hold onto hope

Reach out arms

Sustain yourself as life departs

Reach out arms

Remove vestiges all of love

Reach out arms, reach out

As empty you wait lonely now -

Smile, smile oh lips

The city great in splendour lies

The heart in lonely horror cries

The soul for peace seeks respite

Smile oh lips smile

In cruel empty shallow 'guise

Smile on and on

A fool you shield from all about

Smile oh lips, smile

Let not the world me know about

Smile oh lips smile -- just smile

The Wind and the Rain

(name of person)

The wind and the rain

They call out your name (name of person)

Sometimes in great joy

Sometimes in deep pain (name of person)

The echo it grows it grows

And grows until it shatters

My ears bells are ringing ringing

With the only sound that matters

The sound that haunts my days

The sound that changes my ways (name of person)

The voice that like music rings

The name that to me soft sings (name of person)

What have you done to my heart

What have you done to my dreams

Nothing else e'er gave me a start

Like your voice and presence it seems

Cast you your spell over me

Let my life ring with your joy

Complete for me my destiny

As you in my arms I employ

One moment as soft blows the wind

Singing e'er of you o'er again

(name of person)

Life's truest measure

of a man lies in the degree

of conformity he refuses to accept.

Mirror Liquid Mirror of Beauty

Mirror liquid mirror of beauty

Which reflect last snows of winter

And show first buds of spring

As they both light upon and share

The thick hard foliage of green forest

In rippling sheets unbroken yet

The sheep-like clouds o'erhead scurry

Chased by the silvered red fox

Of evenings sun upon raincloud

But distant yet it is

And distant still remaining

Unnerved each time its image

In direct response it sees

Liquid mirror, liquid beauty

A dressing stage for fish and bird

As each their full attire inspect

Then fast upon their journeys far

One up the other under

They bid farewell to golden sheen

As in the spotlight you prepare

Your clearest mirror for the king who comes

Majestic eagle -- king of all

Majestic eagle you

A-soaring thru the air

Happy the woman of a beautiful exterior

For she may have any man she wants,

&

Happier the woman of an interior beauty

For she can have one who wants her,

&

Happiest the homely woman of charms

For she can rest assured that the man

Who took her hand

He was truly deep in love with her...

Nothingness -- Absolute Nothingness

Nothingness -- absolute nothingness

From here to far horizon

A vast and empty nothingness

From ocean to the stratosphere

From bottom to the top

No break, no mark no anything

This unending nothingness to stop.

Just vast and bright and drear

Just open far and wide

The completeness of nothingness

Seems it alone rides on the tide

No bird, no plane no ship

No tug, no cloud nor smoke

Save but the glow of outbound sun

Naught else in this nothingness float

But stare on fool that I am

Blind careless and unthinking

Unseeing of the splendour which

Lies before me e'er revealing

It's day and light and love and life

It's a vast void, yours to fill

A space in time itself reserved

With nothingness

Awaiting just your will.

Like Two Turtle Doves At Evening Time

Like two turtle doves at evening time

When a summer's day is thru

Like two pools of cool sweet water

After days of deserts hue

Like two buttercups with honey filled

Just a-waiting for a bee

Like truth and love and innocence

All this in thine eyes -- we see.

Weeping Willows, Fir, Pine and Oak

Weeping willows, fir, pine and oak

Surround where you relax

Upon the late green lawn

As Summer's sun gaze downwards

You youth today in joyous thought

With cascade of light brown hair

Like Autumn's leaves hanging down

From the weeping willow near

You grace the grass whereon you lay

The reaches of your skin like sunshine

The greenery of your attire but leaves

Fresh full in bloom by Summer's warmth.

A shadow falls upon you there

'Causing golden flashes to be seen

As nature plays its Summer's sun

Upon the tresses of your hair

Unknown, aye so you are

An mayhap so will e'er remain

An inspiration -- apparition

Which on a Summer's eve appeared

So slight the time you rested

Upon natures pad of comfort

Which warmed by August evening

The grass it had become

And yet, and yet one glance

One moment for a camera shot

To be upon you focused

And you became the object of

This song in a sunlit park

So are dreams dreamth

So are visions seen

Within the eyes of the waiting artist

Who glances up unnoticed by

The subject of his glance

The scene is set the words are writ

The moment ever captured

The song of the Summer park sunlit

Will from now on live forever

See Them Strut Proud in Life's Parade

See them strut proud in life's Parade

Heads held high they show their wares

Forward going

Where no one dares invade

Young and full of life

The Representatives

Like the winds

Which from four quarters blow

So too do they

Four vast regions show

Each unique yet

A twelfth of the whole

Each embarking on that elusive goal

One by wiles

Life's game will play

While soft, silent, subtle is another's way

Laughter while straight out

So is her question thrown

Patience and cunning by is the other known

Varied each like engines

Finely tuned which propel

Size, shapes and designs

Each known so well

Yet the purpose in life

Each remains the same

Playing life's own game -- love --

The Representatives

The weight of a little silence

lies heavy and when suppressed for years

its total mass when broken

could well shatter completely

the world which did compress it.

You're My Last Rose of Springtime

You're my last rose of Springtime

Last rose of Spring

Your eyes they sparkle and they shine

You're my last rose of Springtime

Last rose of Spring

But tho you're late in blooming

I'm so glad that bloom is mine

As the last rays of Spring light

Set upon the land and sea

Awaiting for tomorrow's morn

Summers sun to free

Came you a-shyly blossoming

Right here for lonely me

Like a last rose of Springtime

Last rose of Spring.

Your bouquet of beauty full

I earlier had seen

Tho like a window shopping fool

Thought not to step within

Then as nature's florist

Her spring flowers put away

My eyes met and froze upon

The last Spring rose bouquet

As your petals show their softness

Which below the leaves are pressed

Two silvered dewdrops shining

Stand out from all the rest

And the brocade that envelops

Your perfume it sweetly sends

Soft sweet fragrance

Of a Springtime without end

For your eyes are bright dewdrops

The petals form your lips

While cheeks like leaves warm

Enfold beneath the brocade of your hair

The brocade of your hair

Which keeps your fragrance near

In one single rose of Springtime

You a bouquet I behold.

'Twas Midnight On a Moonlit Eve

'Twas midnight on a moonlit eve

By a calm Pacific shore

I listened as the waters lapped

Wood drifts and rocks all o'er

Then far away across the path

Of moonlights golden sheen

There stood afar -- there stood aghast

The most threatening being I've seen

Back-on he stood, looking out

Towards the dark bleak horizon

Yet forward to me did he come

Each step back a measured sure one

Each step he took a chill it sent

Like winters icy breath

That raze my body to the bone

As I knew I watched here death

My fears were filled to bursting point

My thoughts -- life's past with ran

A solitary cloaked figure he

Reaper grim with outstretching hand

And on he came across the tide

Each step seemed to enshroud

The very waves he walked upon

So upright sure and proud

Yet never once did his face turn

To gaze upon mine blank

And maybe this is reason why

Tonight for life I thank

Each solitary step he took

Backwards which brought him near

Increased within the heart of mine

The meaning full of fear

'Til he reached the nearer shore

And he silhouette there stood

Unable he it seemed to move

Once more his lighted foot

Then glancing up across the tide

Another being 'twas seen

This one shone like a distant light

Like some warning beacons beam

Across the tide unto the shore

In back of where death stood

The beam of life in that light

It, even death full understood

Up went his arms to left to right

His cloak himself enshroud he did

A figure lone in moonlit beam

Unmoving, fully seen, yet hid

And from the reaches of the Earth

A trembling strong 'twas felt

And the piercing cry he let out

By which the night itself was rent

Then fast forward and affront

He steps took with lively gait

Across the moonbeams on the waves

To its end then turned in hate

A bellow-like in rage spewed out

Meteoric flames towards the light

Which with its beacon shining forth

Had robbed him his prey tonight

"In time, in time, in time" he said

"We'll meet I'm sure again

For nothing lives that won't be dead

I'll but once more call you friend."

With that o'er far horizons brink

He left -- my chills and fears were gone

But a skull mark's now upon my chest

First seen there at light of dawn...

Love Is But a Fertile Ground

Love is but a fertile ground
We plant therein the seeds we choose
If they be trust or hope or doubt
From that ground we can but expect
Blossoms of the same to sprout.

Love is but a watery trough
In which we may sink or swim
Thirsty hearts find quenching drink
Others see but the smirk they think
Wallowing there in their mire.

Love is but a passing wind
Catching all the smells that be
With some lingering softly on
Others passing over free
'Less their pungent odours spree.

Love then lives in everything
Earth and water and in wind
In the heart and soul and mind
Waiting but for one to find
Where their niche of Love it hides.

I Walked Along a Sunlit Beach

I walked along a Sunlit beach

In early Autumn eve

And marvelled at the Summer bathers

Laying there in unison with nature

And I for the first of many years

Saw not their natural nakedness

But rather I their beauty full beheld

As awareness and perception

Of the freedom of the body and the Soul

Stood outwards in full freedom

What controversy this I clad did ask

And finding I no answer wandered on

What harm herein or debasement them here to

When they like Earth's first creatures open free

Roamed even now in innocence

Frolicking along the sandy shores

Bare but barred from the public's eye

And seeking naught but freedom to express

As in this wooded habitat they wandered

I traveled on but then it seemed that I

Uncomfortably in my suit of modesty

Could not leave long this call too to be free

To come and join among this happy throng

So casting off my age old morals suit

My garments which now brought me but shame

I entered in among these free as one

And as I did I found one I became

Accepted I and free as man could be

Tho naked I walked unashamedly now with these

A child of nature pure by nature's sea.

My thoughts they ran to morals

My thoughts with questions filled

As man and woman boy and girl

Of ages all I gaze upon unclad

Yet no one stared in horror or concern

Yet no one thought the other to observe

We all as one became as nature planned

We walked we swam we talked we danced

We read we slept we lay upon the ground

Enjoying full the merriment of each other

No inhibitions now to stay our talk

No need for false converse to pass the time

No need for idle chatter while the mind

Roamed thru the eyes the body wandering over

For we were all the same and unashamed

We had reached the higher reaches of humanity

By simple innocent forgotten quirk

We had returned as we at first had been

Just human beings all naked on the Earth

My head it swam in full giddy enchantment

As I in rapture full freedom first realized

As I my last held inhibitions cast aside

And lay face up among a group of ten

A group of ages varied girls and men

Yet felt not I a single sensual urge

My pillow here a log, my legs uncurled

My book an interest in serious I could take

Calm comfortable and at peace within

Such peacefulness I never yet had known

While lying clad by river sea or lake

Thinking thoughts of each opposite passing by

But here at last unclad with all the rest

My mind was clear and free

My Soul found rest...

'Tis Those Who Are of Death Afraid

'Tis those who are of death afraid

That it doth sneak upon

But we who live life without care

It smiles at and moves on

For life and death are states of mind

Wherein we each can wander

In search of truth or solitude

Each a passageway to the other

So let not fear bring unto thee

The call of death thru fate

But rather laugh at all its wiles

And live full life for life's own sake

Then one day when you tired are

And your mental map is filled

You then can cross that precipice

Where death waits silent still

But you alone can make that choice

In answer to its calls

For you alone can hear its voice

When it beckons you leave all

Like thief at night in shadow dark

It waits this being death

But knows that tho you walk nearby

It dares not its hands outstretch

As long as you can gaze full out

At life with will to live

Death must but a bystander be

Death cannot change your will

For only those that fearful tread

With footsteps unsure and wary

Will of their own fear wander in

Deaths arms cold awaiting dreary

'Tis those who are afraid of life

That seek thru fear to die

For greater yet their fear of death

It in draws them passing by.

Oh Crescent Moon

Oh crescent moon

Which hangs like golden pendant

Into the hollow of the neck of maiden fair

Between two hills

Which breasts portray

The cover of the valley

Its body and its sheen

Is but the colours in the dress she wears

And golden bright you hang

As velvet black of night

Falls like a gown from shoulders soft

To rest upon the ground

And darkness of the night draws nigh

As first two stars appears to twinkle by

'Tis not the stars alas that twinkle

But merely it's the sparkle

As she opens bright her eyes

And nature smiles --

Why should it not

When yet upon its cheeks

There lingers the sunset like lipstick she wore

And shared with gentle touch

Upon the face of nature

As day she bad farewell and night hello

Tho she asleep remained in nature's bower

So, hang there crescent moon

Hang down like golden pendant

Upon the neck of maiden fair

For tho I have not gold to share her with

Nor me your power and beauty

To on her bestow

Yet I can look upon thee now and offer

To her everything of value, beneath thy glow

My true undying everlasting love

If Only I Could Find the Place

If only I could find the place

In this vast world to live

Where I would not be hounded for my race

And the sorrows that it gives

If only I could find one place within

This Universe that's free

One place apart -- from hate filled hearts

Once place free of bigotry

If only I could find one place whereat

I there could rest my head

In bough of tree or shade of oak

Or in narrow cold grave bed

Thereto fast would I sojourn

To spend my lasting years

One place that's free, one place for me

One time without my tears

If only I could walk one lonely street

Fear not the trees I meet

Fear not the poles along the road

Nor the potholes beneath my feet

Fear not what lays in every brush

Which across my paths I see

Fear not of these and those lurking there

In hate reaching out at me

If only I could find one place within

This wide wide Universe

Wherein my soul might freely live

Wherein my body not be cursed

Wherein this life of mine could live

And there flourish equal free

If only I could find one place of Peace

Then World -- no more you'd see of me

Then World -- cold cold hate filled world

No more -- no more you'll see of me

White Painted Smoke or Powdered Air

White painted smoke or powdered air
Or gossamer spiders weave
Fairy hair off first born child
Or cloud in late summers eve
Ghostlike silent white and pale
It breathes upon the mirrored waters
Lending its shadowed hue thereto
Life-like like one who ponders
Low below its sky expanse
Low below the hillside
Low below the trees which grow
To grace the sea-lapped shorelines.
Here where water meets the land
To copy, fresco, carve and trace
In mirrored paintings picturesque
Floating or embedded part of the rest
Wisp of wind and scurry starts
Its form not to dissipate
As back upon its journey high
It climbs 'til winds abate
And there it rests with smile formed
High for all to see --to believe
White painted smoke or powdered air
Or web of gossamer spiders weave.

Impatient Youth

Impatient youth -- have you then alas

Your restless spirit freed

Your quest for glamour

Has it all been filled

Your beat of heart in haste

To run while young all life

Your will to do all things

Good -- bad -- wrong or right

So, have you now at last

Your restless spirit freed

If so give heed then to

My call of love to thee

For yet I linger

I linger here yet patient

Until your morn has passed

Until your noonday's sun grows dim

I silent and alone persist

For in thy well of feelings

Once I did dip and splashing

There short, I glimpsed of love

I glimpsed beneath the waters

Which boiled upon the surface

Beneath the muddy turmoil

Which in your "want-to's" lay

I glimpsed there near the bottom

The end of your feelings well

A time of peaceful serenity

Which tried to hide away

And so I've lingered

I've waited in the sidelines

That you freely could walk

Could run, could fall, could play

A distant I, tho watchful

Unseen yet ne'er unseeing

A lover longing lingering

For you one day to say

"Alas at last with spirit freed

With restless heart now restful

With quest for glamour finished

Still resting unfulfilled

Oh soul now show full meaning

Oh life now show true love

If there be one still waiting

I pray thee seek me now"

Impatient youth -- have you then alas

Your restless spirit freed?

The best of metals

when subjected to fire,

heats very slowly and

takes thrice as long to naturally cool

--

so too the best of women

when confronted by man.

Dear Lonely Heart -- Oh Bloody Wonder

Dear lonely heart -- oh bloody wonder

In search of deep divine design

You beat and wander on so eerily

Hoping someway to find what's thine

You seek to reach the open spaces

Where truth and joy and love abounds

You try to reach the painful lonely

With warmth and your vibrating sounds

You who have felt the pain of anger

You whom in tenderness did lay

You who has pained yet never faltered

You who yet sustains my life today

What places do you go to gather

These attributes which make you grand

What price do you pay to gather

Such strength to deal with a fellowman

And as upon life's path you travel

Oh tell me heart if e'er you can

What secrets of life do you unravel

What is your deep and final plan

How long must you sit in silent sorrow

How many pains pray can you take

How hard will hurt make you tomorrow

Or is it true that you can break

Oh heart you seek for love and freedom

You seek to end your loneliness

Yet you endure thru all in wisdom

Surrendering not to unhappiness

Contented ever to keep a-beating

In perfect rhythm throughout time

May you find the peace you're seeking

Dear lonely heart old friend of mine

Why work on? --

because the weight of idleness lays heavy

upon the shoulders of an honest man.

Come Climb With Me

Come climb with me
Up yonder mountain
High above the fjord-like waterway
Beyond where we can see
The last rays of a perfect day
As the sun in golden nest
Splays forth o'er all our world
A myriad of colour in the west.

Come climb with me
Where the timid deer open play
Where the hill pheasant
And the mountain quail
Chuckle as we bypass their trail
Where the tree squirrel squeaks
In perfect rhythm of its moving tail
As if the sounds he's sending out
Comes not from throat or voice
Comes more seemingly from tail than mouth
As the dusk falls upon another day
We yet can catch sun's parting ray

Come climb with me
Above the Islands highest peak
Where below the roads ribbon
Where snake-like rivers become
Where we can the mainland see
In cloudlike haze thirty miles away
Like some gigantic ship afloat
Upon a golden grey green glassy sea
As bath of sunlight like an artists brush
At ending of a perfect piece of art
Goes out to but lend perfection's touch

Come climb with me e'en higher
Where above, the Eagles only dare
Where rests the mighty Malahat's spire
And you and I can rest with nay a care
Come climb with me let nature surround
Our lives as one to there become
The past below we'll leave behind
As higher we the fleeting sunlight chase
'Til there at ocean's farthest edge
I watch it sink -- its glow left on your face
There I will with you in silence wait
Until its sheen has gone at last away
Then taking you soft close in my arms
I taste your lips, ending full our perfect day

Today Tides Choir It Took Rest

Today tides choir it took rest
As not a wave held a crest
And not a bird sang at its nest
Yet all was calm and peaceful
I strolled along the waters side
To hear the music of the tide
Mixed with the birds but I -- surprised
Found natures chorus -- quiet
I waited but 'twas all in vain
I must wait the sounds to hear again
For they play not on without end
In any one location.

A time for triumph and for song
A time to parade and clash along
A time for peace too to be found
Each must be appreciated
I learned the lesson old as time
As I relaxed in peace of mind
Content tho here I did not find
The band of nature's chorus
So resting back my head instead
Upon the pillow log of my sand bed
I watched the Autumn trees slow shed
Their leaves to await the winter.

To Live in the Feel of Fear

God -- to live in fear of life

How lonely it must be

To shut out oneself from all around

And call that living -- free

To look at anyone around

Whom different someway seems

As a danger to ones life itself

Part of an unending horror dream.

To live in fear of life itself

'Cause so much hurt you've shown

You fear from all what you deserve

Should they repay in what they've known

And so in ever wakeful fear

You like stalked prey turn aside

At slightest noise or stranger seen

You feel you fast must hide.

Break out -- break out man and live

Let all peoples equal be

There's none unknown to you who waits

To threaten your life or dignity

There's none unknown to you who will

Harm cause to you thru hate

Tho different may their features be

Tho their skins hue a darker paint

So walk among the world of man

Where once you walked alone

Your only need to fear in life

Is the guilt of past and actions yours

Yet even past is past and gone

The future for all lies free

Walk by the black, brown, yellow or red

He seeks not white man to harm thee

Stay awhile outside and breathe the air

Which on us all blows the same

Be you King or pauper, man or beast

Unknown or of worldly fame

For God -- it's hard to live in fear

As I watch you so unfree

When you like I could walk out to

A full new found eternity.

Judge not then others by their race

Let not their difference cause you fear

This world is theirs and yours and mine

Come join us all free living here.

It was so hot that her cold words and looks...

Became but such welcome gestures

DNC 120894

Sans Luck -- Sans Desperation

Far below the body that you show unto the world

There I ventured and was captured by your heart

Solemn organ beating warm hidden in its fold

Deep deep down where your true beauty starts

So said I my mind to as your mind mine did impress

Take thee heed of this inner beauty rare

For no finer may the linen

be which graces full the bed

Than the peoples deep in love who layeth there.

This vision of thy inner beauty which touches my soul

Soft and warm like sun's caress of dawn

Lay so easy on my mind in works which it atolls

Like soft fresh snow a-falling on a lawn.

This then has no need for a time of desperation

This then has no need of sheer luck to make it real

It but needs affection freely given and received

It but awaits moments of warmth for it can feel.

Deep the heart, secret the mind,

and unknown the soul may be

Hidden all 'neath the body you to the world expose

Judge may they thy body only

as their shallow eyes it sees

Yet your inner beauty rare

few see and far fewer know.

Touch of hand in crossing, signals to the heart

Video-like me thine eyes, thy hidden beauty shows

Unmasked you -- I see beyond your body's outer parts

To deep within your heart, your mind your soul

Yet you appear not desperate even now for life

I stand aback no opportune child of luck to be

You need not wait for luck to ease your inner strife

Nor need I desperation your inner beauty rare to see.

The Morning's Musky Ray of Gold

The morning's musky ray of gold
Paints the damp wet foggy day
As golden crested seagulls soar
O'er an ocean of light grey

They bob and weave we pitch and turn
They rise to heights above
We ever downwards seeming go
To caress the waves with love

Not far away the shoreline wakes
Another day to greet
As night and morning intertwines
And light and darkness meet

The haze surrounding disappears
As the first rays of sun is felt
Burning thru the grey fog cloud
A silvered-golden belt

Then patch of sky in myriad blue
A challenge to the seas appears
The greyish tint of night rolls by
As we breathe the new day's air

Then warmth of life returns again
Reaching to touch us everywhere.

It's Easy for a Lonely Heart

It's easy for a lonely heart

To write hurting words on paper

For it's not ink which flows thereon

But blood streaming from the fingers

The heart that stood, it too may break

After all its agonies and pains

After each outreach for companionship

It finds itself lonely once again

Then miles of tubes straight from the heart

Which pulsed with blood for life

Becomes but reservoirs for the pen

Which of all the hurts and pains must write

This bladder of the pen -- the heart

Outspills its inky content

In words upon a page of life

In destiny's book which we are lent

This then is why it's easy writ

The hurtfulness of the heart

Once filled to bursting like a dam

Takes but small a crack to start

The life and times that make a life

So empty -- cold -- forlorn

Like I have seen a life slow made

Like you have made my own

Thus my words are so easy writ

When of pain and loneliness I write

When I speak of cold and dreary days

Of long empty lonely nights

The end must come, must come to all

And even to this rhyme

The ink -- my blood -- which with I write

Will run out too in time

Then -- only then -- but mayhap then

Alone -- you then may understand

The emptiness you shadowed on

A once happy loving man

In sleep or wake I shall be gone

Out o'er the dark abyss

Where no more hunger shall I know

For the cold touch of your kiss

Yes 'tis easy for a lonely heart

To write words of hurt upon paper

For it's not ink which flows thereon

But hearts blood out thru the fingers

And when my words they soon do end

You'll know happy I have gone

At last free of my pain-filled life

At last no more, no more alone.

Real Pearls

Solitary droplet of dew

Frozen on a wintry limb

A myriad of sunlight's gold array

Shimmer off you yet you remain

Like a hanging pearl set in the wild...

Face of maiden fair soft set

Resting on one cheek you show

Deeper thought than she outwards express

Pearl like tear alone you hang

Like an unset pearl you hang and glow...

Cultured ivory like perfected teeth

Which behind a warming smile is seen

Bursting to express their hidden presence

Waiting warmer yet their gifts to share

Pearl-like? Nay, real Pearls are these.

I've Tried -- I've Tried

I've tried -- I've tried

Dear God I've tried

'Til now alone I stand and cry

I cry out for release

Help for my inner mourning soul

Help for my daily needed toil

Help to go on and to just be

I've cried -- I've tried, Dear God

Help me -- help me.

The lonely emptiness I feel

The cold cold warmth that me deceives

The reaching for what cannot be

The unfeeling looks of destiny

Each time I reach it to hold.

You -- like the dry hard block of ice

The frozen mass of dioxide gas

Which speaks of warmth in smoke

Which speaks of life in jokes

As to the touch you burn

Each fool who to you turns for warmth

You freeze cold all those nearby.

What creature you of nature

Sure surely not a being human

Tho of form human you do seem

Not yet machine -- yet machine-like

Yet indestructible without e'er destroying

You persist to on life evoke -- pain

Your hot burn from your cold touch

Then laugh on -- laugh on as I cry

I've tried -- these years -- I've tried, I've tried

'Til emptiness fills my insides

And defeated at last here I lie.

I lie defeated upon my empty bed

With seeming face upon the head

Which indents the pillow there instead

Of warm flesh and blood and bone

I gaze upon the hollowness

Which like an inflate I caress

So soft to touch this hollowness

This empty shell I could possess

And yet remain would I alone.

I've tried -- I've tried

Dear God -- I've tried

'Til now alone I stand and cry

I cry out for release...

I Stood With Glasses in My Hand

I stood with glasses in my hand

And watched King Neptune give command

To start one wave towards the land

From yonder far horizon

It swelled and swelled

It grew and grew

And from it high the salt spray flew

And I deep wondered what to do

Before it can reach where I am

Yet on and on and on it came

Tossing ships and fishing boats the same

Like a giant quarterback at a game

Would toss around his midget juniors

Still thru my glasses I did watch

Each move it made 'twas mine to catch

Wondering how long before it reached

And burst upon my safety

Then as it onwards came it seemed

That it grew smaller like a dream

Tho rushing onwards with a stream

Of surf arising from it

My eyes stayed opened and fast glued

Unto the glasses I held crude

Which magnified its magnitude

Even more than I imagined

Then I my foot it slipped awhile

A pebble fell and then I smiled

For in the water dark and wild

A ripple it sent over

My glasses fell they from my hand

I watched the beauty near the land

As the giant wave neared the stand

Of shoreline where I'd wandered

Then music soft rose unto me

As the wave met ripple of the sea

And peacefully it sang to me

Of its birth from away out yonder

Each wave we meet it seemed to say

Starts out a ripple on some bay

With naught to worry -- it won't stay

To harm cause the calm onlooker

And chorus then it in did join

With all the waves that lapped around

To sing out loud in peaceful sound

We live but to sing -- forever.

Oh He Rides the Waves Unending

Oh he rides the waves unending

Sails the seas all without bound

Seems without a care or worry he

Long as he's outwards bound.

From port to port From shore to shore

From ship to ship he goes

By every isle or land or reef

Up each river which outflows

His gait is long and staggering

Like a horseman yet unmount

" 'Tis me sea legs that causes it"

He proclaims with prideful pout.

The tales he spins of Netherlands

Which to he all has sailed

The monsters of the deep dark sea

Which to many's a watery grave.

Bronzed by the sun the sea the wind

Like leather feels his cheeks

Yet back the wrinkles of his eyes

One sees twinkles as he speaks.

His laugh is jovial and loud

With patience is he blessed

Contented he upon the sea

He in tranquilly finds rest.

Then shore time comes to him awhile

And there he hastens fast

To formulate some memory new

To add to tales gone past

Like fish out of the water took

He restlessly rolls 'round

Each bar or club or enter spot

He finds in each new town.

One day or two then back he goes

To the one life that he knows

Where sea and salt spray wash his face

As around the world he goes.

He's hooked like some dope addict

He's twisted as some knave

To leave it all has been his dream

Since the time first that he came.

Each storm calls back to memory

Those which he rode in doubt

A-swearing that should he live thru

This time he'd sure pull out

Yet as the winds abate the tide

And smooth the old girl rides again

He looks at her like lover lost

She holds him near as friend

Then snug within her bosomed arms

He feels her life and warmth

Secure as babe upon a breast

Forgetful of the storm

What sickness this -- one often asks

Which calls a man from home

To give his life up to the sea

And to on her billows roam

No sickness this but rather love

Like when man finds a mate

So too a ship calls wanderers home

To gamble e'er 'gainst fate

Each length a ship moves on the sea

Brings it nearer to its grave

Each trip a sailor signs anew

Renews his losing chance again

Yet it's a gamble like all life

And man must make his way

To live on shore with kids and wife

Or on oceans tops to play

Then let me face fate as I've done

Long as a ship sets sail

I'll place my trust in her below

As on and on I'll sail.

Show Me Love and I Shall Live

Show me love and I shall live

Show me hope and I shall will

Show me joy and I shall give

Show me truth and I shall speak

Show me help and I shall stop

Show me justice and I shall ask

Show me life and I shall want

Show me truth and I shall speak

Show me, show me, show me

Show me -- equality

Show me -- equality

Show me equality and I shall die

Nay not a cold quick bodily death

Nor yet a mental anguished call

But one life completed overall

One life fulfilled

One journey ended

One quest reached

One not suspended

One belief freed from ever doubt

One unreachable goal sought out

Show me equality and I shall die

I shall die,

But happy I

For long the search has weary been

Seeking but this from my fellowmen.

7/3/81

I Thought I Had a Friend One Time

I thought I had a friend one time

We did all things together

We sailed, we played each sport there be

In every type of weather

We fished and hunted sang and laughed

And shared a glass of wine

We to each other brought great cheer

In the poor and in rich times

We never seemed to quarrel

O'er things most peoples do

We stood each other firm behind

The tough we saw each other thru

Yet there remained 'tween he and I

It seemed -- a wall -- somehow

Of things unsaid of life and death

Which we spoke not somehow of

Our ways of meeting each day's life

'Twas always not the same

He didn't seem to understand

Man's birthplace brought no shame

Yet thru it all together we

Stayed close onto the end

For somehow here -- I always thought

I thought I had a friend.

I thought I had a friend some time

As we passed the summers thru

We ran and chased we swam and danced

She'd sing a song or two

I'd tell to her my secret thoughts

She with me hers would share

Creating we for times to come

Memories beautiful and so rare

Then one day she just up and left

I don't know where she's gone

She didn't say goodbye or when

Or if, she'd be back my way along

We often held each other's hands

Or sat just side by side

Yet somehow lips -- ours never kissed

Nor a sweetheart love e'er tried

We lived together yet apart

For oh so many many years

A true bosom pal, my friend that gal

Yet no sexuality did we share

Now tho she's gone -- I don't know where

'Tween here and the world's end

I still believe deep down inside

I thought -- I thought I had a friend

I thought I had a friend one time

Who like me humbly grew

And yet it seemed so very strange

This friend I never knew

I knew all there was to know

About Him and of his ways

The things he did the things he said

The way he lived from day to day

I knew what he expected of

Both life and me -- I guess

And somehow -- it just didn't seem

I had need to know the rest

'Tis strange that now I sit and think

Of the friends all I have known

The males, females, those near and far

Who have all come along and gone

Still out front -- this one remains

He seems there all the time

I look up and I see his face

I hear his words in mind

I feel his touch when I need someone

To help me go along

I listen and I hear his words

In faint and distant song

But most of all what I have found

Is that times when I'm in need

He's always there to lend a hand

He is a friend indeed

The others -- some I have forgot

Their names as times gone on

But still his lingers in my mind

In a soft melodic sound

He's called upon each day by man

Some wrong and by some right

From dungeon dark and prison bleak

To church pew with altar bright

And tho at times there passes time

When to him I just don't speak

Yet still within I guess he knows

A loyal friend I try to be

For when I come for help or peace

And solace now and then

I know -- I know -- my Lord I know

In you -- I have a friend.

When First They Met Their Eyes Embraced

When first they met

Their eyes embraced

With such a depth of fellowship

With warmth and love and feeling

Such as they'd never known

Her face aglow

It sparkled light

Yet distant did she keep it

Deep down within a-wondering

Could she be someday his own

The lady loved the poet

But the lady wouldn't show it

So unbeknowing the poet

Walked off in the night alone.

When next they met

The sparkle grew

The poets heart 'twas showing

The lady kept her feelings

Hid in the distance well

Yet in her words

There rang a chime

Of love-bells clearly ringing

And a heart alone and lonely

Loves first echoes heard it tell

The lady loved the poet

But the lady couldn't show it

Tho the lady knew the poet

In his heart too loved her well.

The time it passed

From months to years

Their friendship hit high a peak

They wallowed in the presence

Of each other when they could

Still silent she on loving

Still silent he a-waiting

Each fearful 'less they tread upon

Be it willful or unwilling

Some vestibule where now not they should

The lady loved the poet

Deep she tried so not to show it

While the lady knew the poet

Oh so deep he loved her too.

Then life's dam

It one day opened

Loves waters came a-rushing

Flooding o'er the bounds which held it

Back in check so many years

Arms surrounding

Lips full searching

Heart within with passion pounding

Full the love she'd been denying

Burst full outwards without fears

And the lady loved the poet

Now assured the poet of it

Filling full his heart forever

For he the lady too adored.

So it goes... The lover's story

Of the lady and the poet

Who still keeps their love a secret

'Less the world may disapprove

For he is committed

For she is restricted

As the social mores can't understand

Loves between a woman and a man

Who belonged to someone else before.

Still the lady loves the poet

Is no longer 'fraid to show it

As they together always sparkle

Each moment life to them affords.

The Pub... Home Away from Home Nearby

Home away from home nearby
Warmth of fire and of friends
Books and games upon the wall
Like a homey large rec-room

Bat-like glasses o'er the bar
Hang awaiting blood-like wine
As the chilly fridges breath
Oh so cold the beer blows o'er

Liquor of each kind is stacked
Affront the shiny mirrored wall
Where the cups and jugs are stacked
Awaiting for the patrons call

Then day it breaks from work
In comes the weary traveler
Dirty, tired, beat, alone
Cold from the toil expired

Sit around a table round
Lounge affront the fire
Elbows on the bar support
The ultra lonely worker tired

The gold in liquid form it flows
From the tap to chilly glasses

Each patron two to start requests
Out goes beer to the masses

As alive comes the tables all
Louder grows the chit and chatter
Work and worries of the day
Seems to leave 'til nothing matters

Nothing save the liquid cooling
And the distant music playing
As each in their own contemplating
Drown or wash away their hurting

Like a home away from home
Where a smile of warmth is seen
Tho it may but be commercial
Still it's real and warm in dreams

And so we return the lost and lonely
Here to quench our thirst and trials
Here to seek the fillings needed
Needed to fill our empty innards

Home away from home nearby
Solace for the uncomforted
Peace for the restless wanderer
Pub-lic place for the heart weary
Pub-lic moments in time set free.

I Love You With a Lasting Love

I love you with a lasting love
A feeling which grows with time
A being which within me thrives
And only for thy presence lives.

I love you with a worshipful glance
A fleeting thought, a midnight dream
A memory old often recalled
A song I hear or softly sing.

I love you with a flutter of heart
A breath I hold a gasp I take
An itch I scratch for comforts sake
A reach my arms outwards may take.

I love you with a brush of brow
A wash of hands or warm of feet
A glance into a mirror there
Where you reflected my eyes in I see.

I love you 'cause you are you
And yet so much a part of me
A wish, a dream, a breath a life
In all my existences you I see.

I love you with a lasting love
A feeling which grows firm with time
A being which helps me survive
By being there -- and being mine.

Summer's Gone -- Autumn's Over

Summer's gone -- Autumn's over

Nature's housekeeper's gone away

A spider's weave of dusky white

O'er all of nature plays.

The World is cold -- the furnace out

The dust of frozen clouds has settled

The caretaker must on leave be

As nature's garden goes untendered

The beasts from high atop the hill

Seek low lands warm and dry

The birds relinquish now their nest

As southwards they all fly

Then desolate like a haunted house

Which uncared for for years has lain

The forests, mountains, lakes and streams

Are all dustlike covered thin

It's winters cold and icy breath

Which spans out everywhere

Leaving in her wake the snowy drift

That like dust -- o'er all appears

This season of soft powdery white

Falling slow like cotton ball leaves

From a grey overcast tree on high

Shedding its long held frozen leaves.

Relief the tree feels as it drops

Its curtain o'er all of white

Painting with its dustlike powdery haze

All nature's beauty from our sight

Old man winter is spreading out

O'er land and sea and lake

His mark in time to cover all

'Til away his dust Spring takes

For soon the staff of Natures house

From their vacation shall return

To melt the ice of winters touch

To clear snows dust off everyone

Then green and yellow gold and bright

Again will shine nature grand

As back to work her helpers three

Stretch out their cleansing hand

Old Winter to the far North then

Will return for long a time

'Til Autumns new gold turns to brown

Falling unattended to the ground

Spring 'n' Summers gone... and Autumn's o'er...

Nature's housekeepers have all left...

A spider's weave of dusky white

O'er all of nature plays.

"Loveliest of Creations"

Hail Sun's warmth -- oh you glow of day

Which pales creation itself with thy beauty

Cast but in passing haste

Thine eyes upon me and into mine

Then I shall glow like early mornings sky

In beauty and radiance reflected off of thee

Mortal man I be -- and it is said as such

Should never play in the Gods abode

But I, more cautiousless than that

I cast my fate upon the Goddess' forbidden shores

And there I stand and gaze in awe

And then I speak full words

But my words tho flow they clearly

Tho so full of admiration for your beauty rare

Still my words run fast to say but voice thee this

Tell me oh Goddess but thy name

Then angels chorus of heaven

In celestial sounds cry out

Or so it seems unto mine ears

When words flow from thy mouth
Lips part -- and I behold the nectar
The nectar sweet of their withholding
And I, untasting of yet rest I, satisfied

Could man before, or now, or ever yet again
Upon such perfection as thee ever gaze
Then, aye, and only then say I
I would have to in reincarnation hold belief
For alas how else could any other eyes
Such beauty in any other face e'er see
I gaze and think of ancient times all past
Of wisdom great which Solomon once knew
Then I see why all things else he outcast

When once he'd laid his eyes
Oh loveliest of the heavens
When once he'd laid his eyes
In wonderment on you

And he, to thee, just he I'd quote
But saved instead his words for you

Read, if carest thou,

As they are in Holy Writ:

Songs of Solomon 1:5-11, 6:10-11 and 4:1-7 in the Bible

That you may see

may see

THEE there fully in it.

Chapter 1

5: *I am black, but comely, O ye daughters of Jerusalem, as the tents*
of Kedar, as the curtains of Solomon.

6: *Look not upon me, because I am black, because the sun hath*
looked upon me: my mother's children were angry with me; they
made me the keeper of the vineyards; but mine own vineyard have I
not kept.

7: *Tell me, O thou whom my soul loveth, where thou feedest, where*
thou makest thy flock to rest at noon: for why should I be as one that
turneth aside by the flocks of thy companions?

8: *If thou know not, O thou fairest among women, go thy way forth*
by the footsteps of the flock, and feed thy kids beside the shepherds'
tents.

9: *I have compared thee, O my love, to a company of horses in*
Pharaoh's chariots.

10: *Thy cheeks are comely with rows of jewels, thy neck with chains*
of gold.

11: *We will make thee borders of gold with studs of silver.*

Chapter 6

10: *Who is she that looketh forth as the morning, fair as the moon, clear as the sun, and terrible as an army with banners?*

11: *I went down into the garden of nuts to see the fruits of the valley, and to see whether the vine flourished, and the pomegranates budded.*

Chapter 4

1: *Behold, thou art fair, my love; behold, thou art fair; thou hast doves' eyes within thy locks: thy hair is as a flock of goats, that appear from mount Gilead.*

2: *Thy teeth are like a flock of sheep that are even shorn, which came up from the washing; whereof every one bear twins, and none is barren among them.*

3: *Thy lips are like a thread of scarlet, and thy speech is comely: thy temples are like a piece of a pomegranate within thy locks.*

4: *Thy neck is like the tower of David builded for an armoury, whereon there hang a thousand bucklers, all shields of mighty men.*

5: *Thy two breasts are like two young roes that are twins, which feed among the lilies.*

6: *Until the day break, and the shadows flee away, I will get me to the mountain of myrrh, and to the hill of frankincense.*

7: *Thou art all fair, my love; there is no spot in thee.*

Let the Glow of Your Soft Eyes

Let the glow of your soft eyes

Mingle with the warmth of your smile

Then flash them across sweet lips

To expose bright pearl-like teeth

And I -- mere mortal man alone

In darkness hid from sun of day

Care not if e'er a new days light

I gaze upon in normal way

For my world -- illuminate it shines

Your radiance fills full every nook

My depressive, pain-like weariness flies

As my life and soul you rejuvenate

By lending me but your presence.

Soft as down your fingers fall

Like fairy wings they your arms draw

My skin it crawls as it you touch

So soft so light for but a while

Yet there shines Summer's sun

Its warmth beating down alone on me

Then you speak and birds in chorus

Sing soft 'mongst fragrant Autumn leaves

At night the Harvest moon looks on

A smile like heaven on its face

Yet small it be by mine compared

For I inside am happy free

As joy and life exudes from you

To blossom full and bloom in me

Simply by lending me your Presence

'Twas On Afric's Banks

'Twas on Afric's banks along the Nile

Where culture blended full with man

Where Christ sought freedom as a child

To stay the weight of Herod's hand

'Twas here civil man of the North

For gold and riches later came

To marvel at their learnedness

To chain and bring those men to shame.

Love Me Not for I Was Not Born to Be Loved

Love me not

for I was not born to be loved

But rather I,

the very womb that gave me life destroyed

Love me not

for I was not born for loving

But rather I,

the tender hearts with, was sent to toy

Love me not

for I shall never return that loving

But rather cold

and distant I constant shall remain

Love me not

for love is not mine for the giving

But rather I

have learnt naught save how to best give pain

Love me not

less seems wasted all you have to offer

But rather watch

as I in misery wallow all alone

Love me not

then you will never have to suffer

But rather pity

my wretchedness as I to life atone

Love me not

with heart of glass for it shall soon be shattered

But rather if

you've love to spare cast it out upon my shame

Love me not

deep still inside for I should not have mattered

But rather share

thy tender loves with those who feel the same

Love me not

for I was not born for tender loving

Love me not

less you befall a victim of my ways

Love me not

for once like you I too loved one unloving

Love me not

less you be cursed like I all of your days

Love me not

but let me be unless you can stay forever

To hold and help me close protect me

From mine own evil wicked ways.

She Sits in Spring or Summer

She sits in Spring or Summer

Thru Winter's cold and Fall

To greet the weary traveler

With her sweet Heiltsuk call

She smiles on all around her

In friendship and in warmth

Her needs but to receive back

The smile she gives to all

Her hair by weather straightened

By age it with silver gleams

Yet like a youth at playtime

To all full of life she seems

Her welcome song to any

Who'll listen it will say

We welcome you dear traveler

From your long and weary way.

She asks not save from heaven

But her daily manna flows

Like a flower on the dockside

Her face there ever glows

So many peoples grace her

That a friend she fast becomes

No tepee and no longhouse

No paint, no spear, no drums

She's just an aging Indian woman

Who still sees the good in men

Who has forgotten hatred's power

Thinking not of what has been.

On the docks at Bella Bella

She is there when you arrive

Early morn or eve of daytime

First and last you'll feel her smile

Soft she hums in Hailhzaqvla

With a voice the angels craves

With a feeling that remains

Telling truly that she cares

Seems she has always been there

And one hopes she'll always be

Just the spark of love a-needed

By all those who cross these seas

Hear her voice it rises upwards

Listen to her rising sound

Listen to her fond reminders

Of what lies 'way out beyond

Hear her stories of the ages

Greetings anew to all she sees

Sending warmth out in her chanting

Drifting softly up to thee

Now the peoples are returning

To their ship for other shores

Many here will see 'gain never

But her tune they'll carry o'er

Like a bird that's sweetly singing

In a tree so bright and gay

Lends to nature fullest splendour

So her voice touches the bay

Now she waves 'seems individual

To each man woman and child

And to each her tune's repeated

As to each she sends her smile

Wafting on the air you hear it

In the dark, the sound, it glows

It's her smile turned into music

In her tune when by you go

It's a hello and a farewell

It's a love song and a tale

It's a chant or it's a liturgy

But it's Josie's heart which wails

Sing on Josie let us listen

Long your song rest in our hearts

You who gives your all, we love you

Thinking of you e'en when apart

Hearing ever your sweet voice echo

In your sweet and warming song

Knowing it gives us safe passage

Protects us all as we sail on.

Ha! Ha! Oh Death

Ha! ha! oh Death

And now alas oh death

I at last can look at thee and laugh

For here within my grasp

Within my arms my reach

I hold the firm and warm fulfillment of my heart

And thus, oh Death, I at last can laugh again

I feel alive and loved

And know now I

That you can not me touch

And so at you I laugh, I laugh

I face my days and night

I mirror full myself and smile at me

For you cannot me touch.

Oh Death how oft for thee I called

In empty desperation I to thee turned

With nary a word or answer lent in help

And only full your smile o'er me

Your smile of cold desperation

And I believed that you

That you and you alone could help

But now I know -- I find that life has hope

For life has love, and in such love a place

A place of warmth -- for me

And so I live again -- And so I love again

And so my heart beats warm

My pulse it races -- my blood boils

As the smile of life upon my lips return

And I laugh at you and all your empty nothingness

Your nothingness which I deep once enveloped in

Have now all changed in full

For joy, for peace, for hope,

But mostly oh death -- I've changed

I've changed forevermore for love

Love, Love which envelops me so softly now

That now alas oh Death

I at last can look at thee and laugh

For here within my arms

Within my grasp my reach

I hold the firm the warm fulfillment of my heart.

To Soar, to Soar, to Soar Like a Bird

To soar, to soar, to soar like a bird

To scream like a demon from Hell

To spread e'er your arms

In motionless flight

As you traverse the heavens in sight.

To know that the wind

Is powerless now

Your journeys to stay or obscure

As above the green valleys

The high rolling hills

The blue of the waters you move...

To soar, to soar, to soar like a bird

To scream like the devil himself

Like an eagle intent

On your way fast you've spent

Motionless you move thru the sky

The roar of your engines

Sweet music it gives

Far louder than a lion can try

You roar, for you rule the Universe true

You scream for yours is the sky.

To soar, to soar, to soar like a bird

To scream like a demon from Hell

The wonders of nature

Man cunningly defies

As in mind bending weight on you fly

Oh but once to again join

Your miles and your route

To fly there on high and be heard

To dream that your wings

My arms are instead

While freely I'll soar like a bird...

I'm Alone and You're Alone

I'm alone and you're alone

Tomorrow we can to life atone

But for tonight -- let's make love.

You are his and she is mine

Yesterday they did suit us fine

But for tonight -- let's make love.

You must go and so must I

We together leave or say goodbye

But for tonight -- let's make love.

Let's cast away our yesterdays

Put tomorrow's movements all on stay

Be you and I in our own way

But for tonight -- let's make love.

Let's ask not who our chains may hold

What might have been our shiny goal

We can write a story later told

But for tonight -- let's make love.

Come into my warm waiting arms

I'll rest contented in your charms

Our lives this night secure from harm

As the long night thru -- we make love

Once more I'm alone and you're alone

Tomorrow we can to life atone

But for tonight...

Just for tonight...

Let's make love...

Let's make love...

Let's make love.

A Short Life

Life consists of 60-90 seconds of time

1 - 10 = 10 sec to be a child

10 - 20 = 10 sec to be a teen

20 - 30 = 10 sec to chart a course

30 - 40 = 10 sec to replace oneself

40 - 50 = 10 sec to guide our replacement

50 - 60 = 10 sec to redo our mistakes

60 - 70 = 10 sec to look back in joy or regret

70 - 80 = 10 sec to contemplate the last

10 sec if we are given them.

So live it now...

I Was Down and Out

I was down and out

In despair and doubt

'Til you came my way

You changed my world

And made me whole

In your sweet loving way

You gave to me, the strength to be

The man I long wanted to

My confidence renewed again

When you gave me you

You gave me everything

You gave me everything

You gave me everything

When you gave me you

You gave me everything

That I needed then

To renew my life

Took all my fears

Removed all my doubts

You made it all right

When I needed help

To feel alive again

Your love came thru

Like a bright shining star

From the heavens afar

You gave me everything

When you gave me you

One Nude -- Two Nude -- One Hundred Clad

One nude--

two nude--

One hundred clad

Then why the controversy

Quite surely all of us at times

Has seen another naked body

The human body beauty has

Such as it's long been graced with

So if bare they choose...

...The sun to embrace

More peace 'n' power to 'em.

Bunny... If Yesterday Today or Tomorrow Calls

BUNNY...

If yesterday -- today or tomorrow calls

And loneliness comes visiting your life

If ever you should need a friend at all

Call on me and I'll be by your side.

If ever you should glance upon the seasons

As they change with every passing day

And like the changing seasons you have reason

To glance back and wish to change today.

If ever your heart it feels a flutter

Or nights feel empty lost and alone

Remember some other one too is lonely

And wishes still you were yet their own.

If ever life should cast your lovely eyes on

The hills, the rivers and the world around

Just think of all their beauty --

Which you brought me

Each time I saw their splendour --

In you abound.

If ever we should cross our paths in future

Cast not thine eyes on mine in silent thought

But rather give me music of your sweet voice

And share a moment short -- a moment ours.

If ever I should walk along life's byways

And see you there in spirit or in truth

You'll know my heart is filled with remembering

The happy happy hours spent with you.

So go on love

And may life be a smile... Yours

Go seek that which

We can't now fully share

Yet find the end of all your hearts desires

And o'er it all you'll see our memories there

If yesterday -- Today or perhaps tomorrow

You find a need to find that saying true

"You're nobody (bunny) 'til somebody (bunny) Loves you"

You're the biggest Bunny love --

For -- I Love You --

Dec/80

Forever -- Poet -- Aye Ever

Forever -- aye ever

I would but live and die

And have bestowed upon me

Nay neither fortune now or fame

Which would one penny place

Within my empty pockets

Nor add one single syllable to my name

But e'er instead just let me be

The roamer free as I've become

The spirit who calls all earth home

And no land nor lady fair hold me a prisoner

And let me traverse as I would

O'er Canada's bounteous shores

'Cross Europe's bleak cold skies

Or out upon the Carib's waters laze

Each stop but choice my own.

Then I shall happy feel and be

Then I all riches and all fame

With, could not replace the warmth

Which would exude from but a smile

As I laugh at the passing world

Nay fortune -- 'tis but gold and silver

Made but to give fools fantasy of life

While demanding interest high in worry

As slowly one watches it slip away

Or cold, useless and unused greater grow

Then at the end in grasp for life

In deep regrets for having had it all

Away you float into the realm

The outer world, the realm of Nothingness

And all your fortunes it remains

Upon the ground where once you wandered

But you -- you empty handed

You are gone

Gone to but watch as overhead

It -- you fortune -- is so lightly spread

And you can only lay

With daisies -- thousands of daisies

Slowly -- silently growing overhead

But I -- ha - ha - ha -- the happy

The carefree and mayhap unknown

I, that skipped so lightly by

As on you toiled

I, whom once a fool

A spendy vagabond of life you said

Would sooner starve than toil and save

For more than daily bread

I -- ha - ha - ha -- I'm yet alive

I'm free -- and still I cling

Tho older now -- my wit and wisdom

They but sharper have become

As I -- as even now I yet survive

I travel and I stop awhile and write

Not words of favour politic

Nor words of hymn for sale

Nor even words of wisdom do I write

But I of life, each picture that I treasure

In words of rhyme these I put down

In simple plain unflowered way

Each one a glimpse into my life each day

Each one holding deep a message

A truth of life that some will see

A call to freedom -- to be free

To live with nary a worry, nor of fame

Nor yet of fortune added to my name

Tho many times the opportune did come

I smiled, and seeing the price so high

I laughed and nodding turned away

For I've alas no fortune, there is none

My many words I've writ no pennies brought

Much of my works still go unsought

I walk the street where few know my name

Yet -- had I life to relive

I'd do it all again -- the same

For I have lived and been happy and free

Without life's fortunes or fames for me

But joy, and life and love I have know

And ask but this as I walk out alone

Upon the stone which marks a humble plot

No epithet of fame have I e'er sought

But I shall rest in peace whene'er I go

If upon my stone one solitary word you show

Then all the world will know

My life from start to end

If large beneath my name

' P-O-E-T '

You do inscribe my friend.

Out Beyond Our Blue Tomorrow

Out beyond our blue tomorrow

Where our pathways narrow down

There's a golden new day shining

Spreading gold upon our ground

Out beyond our blue tomorrows

As our footsteps slower fall

We will see there our tomorrows

Waiting there with beckoning call

We will leave the dreams we once held

All our hopes of days gone past

All our castles in the sand will

Be behind us in our past

We will walk that narrowing roadway

Hand in hand together then

But one dream reserved forever

Guiding onwards to the end

Out beyond the blue tomorrow

Fields of green beneath our feet

Daisy's gold amongst the clover

As we traverse on to meet

Out there where our new day's dawning

Where our twilight times begin

We will walk on slow forever

We together -- lovers -- friends

We will leave all of our charges

On our own we'll life pursue

As we walk that final roadway

Hand in hand just me and you

Out beyond our blue horizon

Where golden paths, ours narrow grow

We will see around that corner

Our dream of Peace at last we'll know

Conversation is a two way street

thereby requiring input from both directions

but wary ever to avoid a head-on collision.

Liberating Lady

Liberating Lady

Hold me not in thy anger

For all of life's frustrations

'Gainst the man I too did share

Life's pains and its heartaches

Its triumphs and disasters

Each a hidden memory

From someone who didn't care.

Liberated Lady

Hold me not in thy accusing

'Less you soon forget me

And the trials I've been thru

You and I are different genders

You and I are different colours

But 'tis these our very differences

Which equates so me and you

Liberated Lady

Hold me not in thine revenges

For to do so would be folly

When together we should strive

If we form a coalition

To battle wrongs we've been facing

Then the man would have to listen

Realize we must survive.

Liberated Lady

Hold me not in thy scorning

For thruout all history

You and I have shared the same

We get less of what is ours

We must give more never ending

Both to the man prostrating

Just to stay here in his game.

Liberating Lady

Hold me not in thy anger

I am not your enemy

I am but your equal friend

Let us stand against oppression

From the ignorant and white man

Then you the female

Me the Black man

Will see equality at the end.

If Ever I Should Leave Thee

If ever I should leave thee

I should leave the tree wherein

We built our nest among its branches

If ever I should leave thee

I should leave our flowing bubbling

Stream whereof we daily sip

If ever I should leave thee

I should leave the music which so

Softly floats around me

If ever I should leave thee

I should leave my hat and coat for

I would be without existence.

If ever I should leave thee

I should leave the chirping voices

Of youth we did create

If ever I should leave thee

I should find no cause for all my

Written words to take

If ever I should leave thee

I should walk away empty, 'lone

And set you free

If ever I should leave thee
I should cease a visible living
Reality to be

If ever I should leave thee
I should leave all I have in
Life attained
If ever I should leave thee
I should be proud if still on you
Bear my name
If ever I should leave thee
I should restrict my future yours
Yet to be
If ever I should leave thee
I should care no longer what
Becomes of me

So bid me stay
Bid me wait a while with thee
Bid me be the one you love
The one who is all he lives to be
Bid me live -- and I shall live
Bid me breathe -- and I shall breathe
Bid me rest in worship at thy feet

And I shall gladly, love, there be

For deep thy life has touched me

My heart and soul soars to thee

My mind and thoughts are on thee

My voice my song my laugh my call

All bear upon them ever loud

Naught but the fragrance of thy name

So bid me stay

Bid me stay awhile

Bid me stay awhile with thee

For if ever I should leave thee

I should not take one little thing

Away with me

For if ever I should leave thee

I should not care for anything

Life past gave unto me

For if ever I should leave thee

I should reject all beauty which

We did possess

For if ever I should leave thee

I should lay claim again on

Naught by emptiness

For if ever I should leave thee

I should leave thee even as thou

Art and has been

For if ever I should leave thee

I shall leave thee to follow death yet

Still be thy friend

And I shall leave thee

Faith and Hope

And I shall leave thee

Peace and Joy

And I shall leave thee

Girls and Boys

And I shall leave thee

Gaiety and Laughter

And I shall leave thee

Fond Memories

And I shall leave thee

All my Possessions

For if ever I shall leave thee

Still tho gone -- Apart or dead

I shall leave thee always

My Undying Love.

Hail Then to Thee Thou Daughter of Aphrodite

Hail then to thee
Thou daughter of Aphrodite
Bedecked in blouse and skirt
Of soft chiffon and of lace
With colourful blossoming Can-Can
Spread out around trim ankles
Which proceed upwards ever upwards
From glass-slippered diamond studded petite feet
To form in the abyss of wonder
Swanlike legs wrapped in downs soft cover and perfume
And I -- aye I --
The jester of the court of fools called Man
I stand alone in dark of night
Like armoured knight of old
Full clad in cumbersome armour
Which shackle seemingly e'en my tongue
My tongue -- which would but wish
In words to bid thee hail
To whisper yet
Deep hearted thoughts and fantasies
Of how a nest of your Can-Can I'd make
And like a bird in early Spring
Fly there into would I in haste
To nestle in among the limbs
The branches of that heavenly tree
Which supports that flowery nest.

4/11/81

The Long Dreary Night Is Over

The long dreary night is over

As here again I sit and think

While my cold and weary body

Rests tired, empty and alone

My thoughts turn to you asking

Is it wrong -- is it wrong?

Is it wrong if I should touch you

As you pass so near to me

With nary more than a quick sweet smile

Is it wrong if I should want to

Just hold your hand in mine

And live in my fantasies awhile

Is it wrong -- is it wrong?

Is it wrong if I should press near

Your warm wet and welcome lips

And savour the nectar I see there

Is it wrong if my fingers wander

To trace the outline of your face

And crawl soft and slowly thru your hair

Is it wrong -- is it wrong?

Is it wrong if I should hold you

Press your warm body close to mine

Feel again the warmth a woman gives to a man

Is it wrong if I should hold you

In sweet embrace a long long time

Then once more desire to hold you so again

Is it wrong -- is it wrong?

Is it wrong for me to whisper

Loving words I've longed to say

Hoping they'll fall in favour on your ear

Is it wrong to foresee a future

With you ever by my side

Living, loving, sharing everyday

Is it wrong -- is it wrong?

Is it wrong, is it wrong I silent ask you

As approach my space you do

And I see your ever shy smile quick appear

Is it wrong -- if not then tell me

In some little thing you do

And in your next step taken

I'll be there --

Yet again I wait and wonder

Silent as you pass me by

'Til another lonely empty day is thru

As the long night passes by

Here I sit again and think

While my cold and weary body

Rests tired, empty and alone

My thoughts turn again asking of you

Is it wrong -- Is it wrong?

Is it wrong?

I'm Your Fantasy -- Live Me

You look at me

Then you glance away

Your eyes hold back

What you lips would say

You think, best wait another day

But -- I'm your fantasy

I'm your fantasy

I'm your fantasy -- live me

You pass by me

You touch my hand

The feelings express

Your deep demands

But you still don't understand

That -- I'm your fantasy

I'm your fantasy

I'm your fantasy -- Live me

Lead me on Lead me on

Show me your wants

Carry me, carry me,

Or come into my arms

Don't hold back with your sweet charms

For -- I'm your fantasy

I'm your fantasy

I'm your fantasy -- Live me...

As You Sit in Your Vestibule

As you sit in your vestibule

Of the mighty house of Lords

Where you seek to legal lead your fellowman

As you think of what is needed

In these days of soft revolt

Think back on ages lived by elders of our land

As you sit and solve the problems

Which today holds youth in check

And the actions which are taken, pray, you think

Are the answers to be found in

All the changes that we make

Or are they found in legalizing dope and drugs and drink

Has the elders in their wisdom

Given causes you to uphold

Or instead perhaps a cause to change

Have their workings of society

Such as we have come to know

Struck you as degenerate and strange

Did you ever see the insides

Of a war-torn countryside

And its peoples cold and starving

On its streets

Have you ever known the feelings

Of just hopelessness and doubt

And see hatred in every eye you meet

Can you lay at night unsleeping

Seeing nightmares passing thru

Of babes crying out at milk-less breasts

Can you picture one of seven young

To full manhood getting thru

Having helped to bury all the rest

May today's youth give you comfort

As you share their troubled joys

And try to better even yet their lot

But as you sit there working hard

In their stead for better lives

Pray teach them to give thanks

For all they've got

As you sit in your vestibule

Of the mighty house of Lords

Where you seek to legal lead your fellowman

As you think of what is needed

In these days of soft-revolt

Think back, think back to elders of our land.

1981 Youth Parliament Nov

For no one has ever

the qualifications

required for any position

without at sometime having been

given the opportunity

to prove their ability.

Wishes They Don't All Come True

Sweetheart
Wishes they don't all come true
Nor are dreams all realized
Yet thru disappointments of the years
I still see me in your eyes
Could that reflection which I see
Be what I look forward to each day
Be those innermost thoughts of love
Be the 'I love you' you do not say

I hope it is and long will last
That sparkle long seen in your eyes
That message silent from the heart
Which fools like me don't realize

Or mayhap I am blind of eyes
By love for you which ever grows
By day by week by month by year
Each moment stronger heaven knows

Why question now our many years
Which knew more joy than sorrow
Perhaps 'tis cause my deepest fears
Would be to face without you -- tomorrow
Love ever yours 1979

(to Grace on anniversary card)

<u>I've Thought and Now I Know</u>

I've thought and now I know

That if I am to love again

I know it can't be now

I still would like to see you

I don't mean this as an end

But if I do -- the circumstance

Can only be as friend

But don't blame me for trying

Guess I haven't grown enough

To accept new ways of thinking

I know that this' so tough

To say --

I know --

We could --

You care --

And even -- I --

Tho you're thoughtful

I feel -- I must be careful

I do not mean to hurt you

If you really care

As you say -- but -- for now

For now I must say

Adieu --

Oh please think on what I say.

<u>Other Collections By This Author:</u>

A Poet's Ebb And Flow

...and Touches Of Nature

In The Middle of Believe There's A Lie

Inside A Heart

Judge Me Not Without A Trial

Legends, Lives & Loves Along the Inside Passage

Love's Reflections

Love's Refuge and Sonnets

Only Children Of The Universe Are We

Step Scenes Of Life

That We Too Free May Live

~ ~

For more information go to:

w w w . d n c s i t e . c a

~ ~

www.ingramcontent.com/pod-product-compliance
Lightning Source LLC
Chambersburg PA
CBHW070807100426
42742CB00012B/2287